nourish _ move _ rest

NOTEBOOK Grid

CROWN

Every Day

nourish _ move _ rest
NOTEBOOK Grid **CROWN**

First Edition

visit amazon.com books to browse current covers and buy
more **nourish move rest** collection online

SHOP   ENJOY   GIFT   SHARE

Instagram  **nourish_move_rest** to share the

ENJOY   LIKE   FOLLOW   SHARE

This publication has been lovingly prepared in good faith, with
due care. The publisher believes that all information supplied in
this book is correct at the time of printing. The publisher is not
however in a position to make any guarantee to this effect and
accepts no liability in the event of: any use or misuse by you or
any person, or any information proving inaccurate. While
endeavoring to ensure reasonable accuracy, the publisher
cannot be held responsible nor liable for any errors or omissions.
No part of this publication may be reproduced, stored in a
retrieval system, modified, adapted, nor transmitted in any form or
by any means, electronic, digital, technological, photocopying or
otherwise, without the prior express written permission of the
copyright holder. Please enjoy wholeheartedly and use in good
faith as a starting point for you. Find your own true path.

" Be aware of your **thoughts**,
They become your intentions.

Be aware of your **intentions**,
They become your words.

Be aware of your **words**,
They become your actions.

Be aware of your **actions**,
They become your habits.

Be aware of your **habits**,
They become your character.

Be aware of your **character**,
It becomes your destiny.

Be aware of your **destiny**,
It becomes your life. "

~ attributed to **His Holiness the Dalai Lama**

Be aware of our shared quality of life

If I may I add, with deep and sincere humility,

" Be aware of your **life**,

It becomes your legacy "

💚 **Every Day**

Every moment is a choice

Ask yourself, **What is next for my best**

Body | **Mind** | **Spirit** | **Mood** | **Stamina**

May your positive impact ripple further…

3Week **WELcome**   more **NOURISH | MOVE | REST**

Take charge & transform your health & fitness regime.
3Week Workbook. Observe & refine your diet & exercise habits.
Rate & improve your overall wellbeing. Be kind to yourself.
WELcome Pages give you step- by- step notes to get started & make positive changes. [These opening pages are only in **WELcome**].
NOURISH Pages become your Food Diary, designed to encourage more mindful & healthy eating. Specific & important questions to gauge how well nourished you feel, every day.
MOVE Pages become your Exercise Journal, empowering you to test & track your fitness & exercise habits. Balanced & targeted ways to get you really moving, every day.
REST *Check in* daily, weekly, regularly throughout your chosen weeks. Continue to challenge yourself, with kindness.
Side- by- side, NOURISH + MOVE [+ bonus REST] pages, every day.
Day To View format. *Bring home **your own health retreat lifestyle***.
Be inspired to welcome your most amazing you! Choose your 3Weeks.
Much love 💜 *Every Day*

4Week **CHALLENGE**   more **NOURISH | MOVE | REST**

Take the CHALLENGE! **Continue** NOURISH | MOVE | REST in colour or black & white option, Food Diary & Exercise Journal side- by- side, familiar *Day To View* format. Choose your 4Weeks.
More love 💜 *Every Day*

8Week **EXERCISE Journal**   more **NOURISH | MOVE | REST**

For those who may need to **focus** on their MOVES [+ REST] before taking a more holistic approach. *It's all inter-related.* Choose your 8Weeks.
Love 💜 *Every Day*

8Week **FOOD Diary**   more **NOURISH | MOVE | REST**

For those who may need to **focus** on their NOURISHMENT [+ REST] before embracing a holistic approach. *It's all good.* Choose your 8Weeks.
Love 💜 *Every Day*

2020 **LIFESTYLE Diary**   more **NOURISH | MOVE | REST**

Make NOURISH | MOVE | REST your *lifestyle*! Fresh format, square *Week To Page*, more to enjoy! *Calendar Year Diary 2020* 12Months.
Love always 💜 *Every Day*

NOTEBOOKS

more **nourish_move_ rest**

Chakra	Colour	Body Location	Element Association	Life Impact & Influences
8 **SPACE**	White Black Grey *No Colour*	Aura *Beyond boundary of body*	Universe	Embrace, Connection, Equanimity
7 **CROWN**	Violet	Crown *of Head*	Ether	Freedom, Meditation, Spirituality
6 **VISION**	Indigo	Mind	Air >> *Light Speed*	Thoughts, Intentions, Mindfulness, Knowledge, Perception, Ideas
5 **TRUTH**	Blue	Throat	Air >> *Sound Vibrations*	Communication, Clarity, Truth, Voice, Song, Storytelling
4 **HEART**	Green	Spirit	Wood *Plants* *Seeds* *Fruit* *Flowers*	Nature, Peace, Sentient Beings: People, Animals, Plants, Rocks Life, Life Force, Growth, Life Cycles
3 **YUMMY**	Yellow	Belly	Fire	Energy, Sun, Stamina, Food Furnace
2 **SACRAL**	Orange	Mood	Water *Feelings*	Emotions, Mood, EI **E**motional **I**ntelligence, Relationships
1 **BASIC$**	Red	Seat *Contact point with the Earth*	Earth	Grounded, Foundation, includes Financial

NOTEBOOKS   each **Blank | Lined | Grid**   ♥ *Every Day*

Instagram    nourish_move_rest

more **nourish move rest** collection   **amazon.com** books

ENLIGHTENMENT

" Before enlightenment,
Chop wood, carry water.
After *enlightenment,*
Chop wood, carry water. "
~ Zen Buddhist Proverb

nourish_move_ rest 💚 Every Day

nourish_ move_ rest 💚 Every Day

nourish_ move_ rest  Every Day

next for my best Body | Mind | Spirit | Mood | Stamina

nourish_move_ rest 💚 Every Day

nourish_move_ rest 💚 Every Day

nourish_move_ rest ❤ Every Day

nourish_move_ rest 💚 Every Day

nourish_move_ rest 💚 Every Day

nourish_move_rest 💚 Every Day

nourish_move_ rest 💚 Every Day

nourish_move_rest 💚 Every Day

nourish_ move_ rest 💚 Every Day

nourish_move_ rest 💚 Every Day

next for my best Body | Mind | Spirit | Mood | Stamina

nourish_move_rest 💚 Every Day

next for my best Body | Mind | Spirit | Mood | Stamina

nourish_move_ rest 💚 Every Day

nourish_move_rest ❤ Every Day

nourish_move_ rest 💚 Every Day

nourish_move_rest 💚 Every Day

nourish_move_ rest 💚 Every Day

nourish_move_ rest 💚 Every Day

nourish_move_rest 💚 Every Day

nourish_move_ rest 💚 Every Day

nourish_move_rest 💚 Every Day

nourish_move_ rest 💚 Every Day

nourish_move_rest 💚 Every Day

nourish_move_ rest 💚 Every Day

nourish_move_ rest 💚 Every Day

nourish_move_ rest 💚 Every Day

next for my best Body | Mind | Spirit | Mood | Stamina

nourish_move_rest 💚 Every Day

nourish_move_rest 💚 Every Day

nourish_move_rest 💚 Every Day

next for my best Body | Mind | Spirit | Mood | Stamina

nourish_move_ rest 💚 Every Day

nourish_move_rest 💚 Every Day

next for my best Body | Mind | Spirit | Mood | Stamina

nourish_move_ rest 💚 Every Day

nourish_move_ rest 💚 Every Day

nourish_move_ rest 💚 Every Day

nourish_move_ rest 💚 Every Day

nourish_move_ rest 💚 Every Day

nourish_move_ rest 💚 Every Day

nourish_move_ rest ❤ Every Day

nourish_move_ rest 💚 Every Day

nourish_move_ rest 💚 Every Day

nourish_move_rest 💚 Every Day

www.ingramcontent.com/pod-product-compliance
Lightning Source LLC
Chambersburg PA
CBHW050751290526
45792CB00008B/2139